Ten well-known carols for young pianists

MYRNA STENT

Kevin Mayhew

We hope you enjoy *Christmas with Max*.
Further copies of this and the other books in the series
are available from your local music shop.

In case of difficulty, please contact the publisher direct:

The Sales Department
KEVIN MAYHEW LTD
Buxhall
Stowmarket
Suffolk IP14 3BW

Phone 01449 737978
Fax 01449 737834
E-mail info@kevinmayhewltd.com

Please ask for our complete catalogue of outstanding Instrumental Music.

First published in Great Britain in 1997 by Kevin Mayhew Ltd.

© Copyright 1997 Kevin Mayhew Ltd.

ISMN M 57004 105 3
ISBN 1 84003 040 2
Catalogue No: 1400141

1 2 3 4 5 6 7 8 9

The music and illustrations in this book are protected by copyright
and may not be reproduced in any way for sale or private use
without the consent of the copyright owner.

Front cover design by Graham Johnstone
Original illustrations: Roy Mitchell

Music Editor: Nicola Greengrass
Music setting by Daniel Kelly

Printed and bound in Great Britain

Contents

		Page
God rest you merry, gentlemen	Traditional English melody	11
Good King Wenceslas	from *Piae Cantiones* (1582)	14
Jingle bells	James Pierpont	6
Lullay, thou little tiny child	from *The Pageant of the Shearmen and Tailors* (1534)	10
O come, all ye faithful	John Francis Wade	13
Sleigh Bells	Myrna Stent	15
Snowball Fight	Myrna Stent	7
The Bells Ring Out	Myrna Stent	12
We three kings	John Henry Hopkins	8
We wish you a merry Christmas	Traditional English melody	16

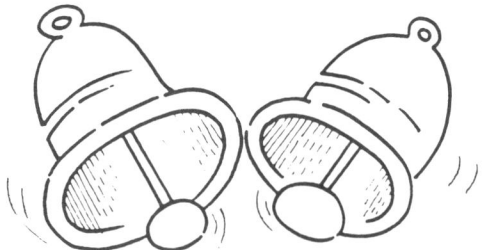# JINGLE BELLS

Allegretto

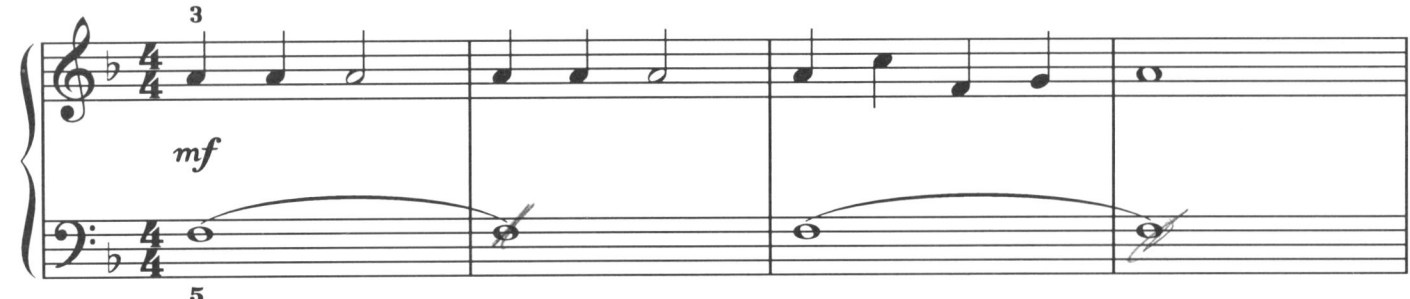

Jingle bells, jingle bells, jingle all the way;
oh, what fun it is to ride in a one-horse open sleigh!
Jingle bells, jingle bells, jingle all the way;
oh, what fun it is to ride in a one-horse open sleigh.

© Copyright 1997 Kevin Mayhew Ltd.
It is illegal to photocopy music.

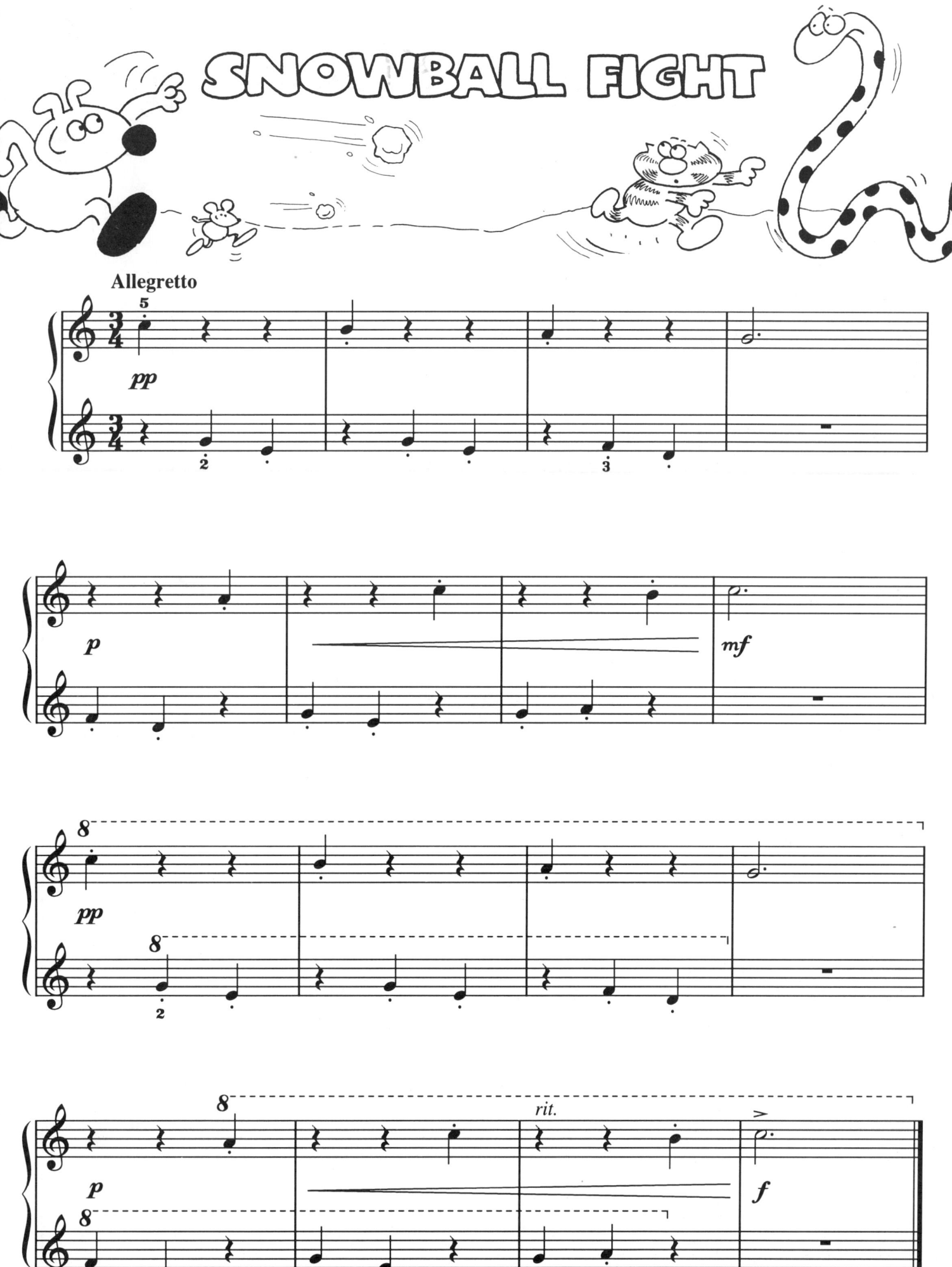

WE THREE KINGS

© Copyright 1997 Kevin Mayhew Ltd.
It is illegal to photocopy music.

We three kings of Orient are;
bearing gifts we traverse afar;
field and fountain, moor and mountain,
following yonder star.
O star of wonder, star of night,
star with royal beauty bright,
westward leading, still proceeding,
guide us to thy perfect light.

Lullay, thou little tiny child,
bye-bye, lullay, lullay.
Lullay, thou little tiny child,
bye-bye, lullay, lullay.

© Copyright 1997 Kevin Mayhew Ltd.
It is illegal to photocopy music.

God rest you merry, gentlemen,
let nothing you dismay,
for Jesus Christ our Saviour
was born on Christmas day,
to save us all from Satan's power,
when we were gone astray:
O tidings of comfort and joy, comfort and joy,
O tidings of comfort and joy.

© Copyright 1997 Kevin Mayhew Ltd.
It is illegal to photocopy music.

# THE BELLS RING OUT
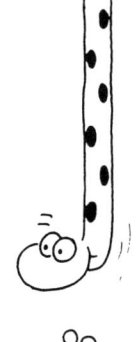

Play both hands an octave higher than written

Allegretto

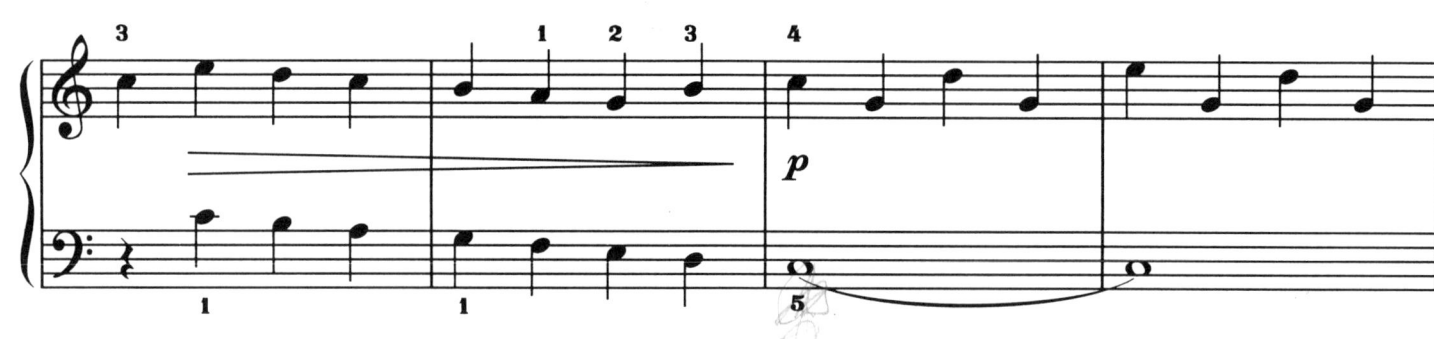

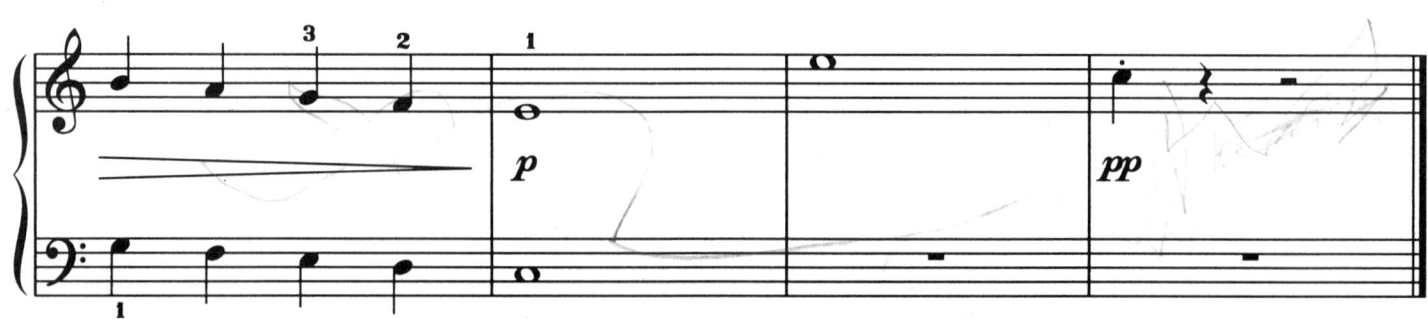

© Copyright 1997 Kevin Mayhew Ltd.
It is illegal to photocopy music.

O COME, ALL YE FAITHFUL

Moderato

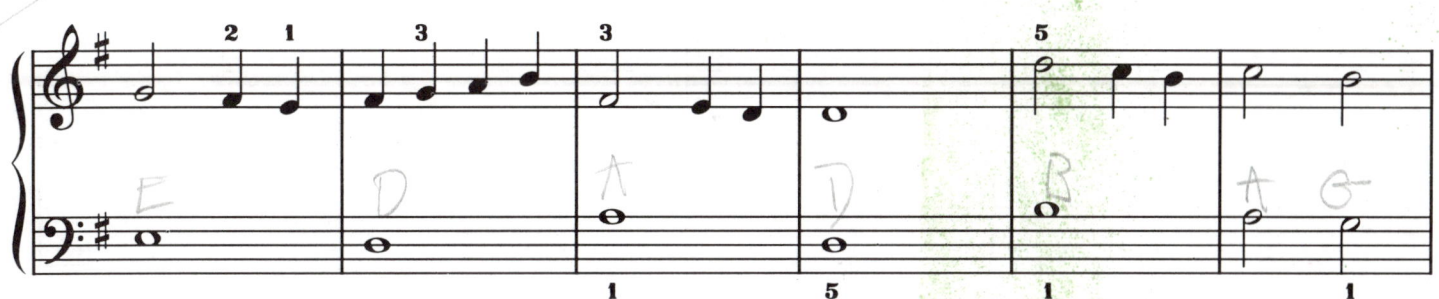

O come, all ye faithful, joyful and triumphant,
O come ye, O come ye to Bethlehem;
come and behold him, born the king of angels:
O come, let us adore him,
O come, let us adore him,
O come, let us adore him,
Christ the Lord.

© Copyright 1997 Kevin Mayhew Ltd.
It is illegal to photocopy music.

Good King Wenceslas looked out
on the Feast of Stephen,
when the snow lay round about,
deep, and crisp, and even:
brightly shone the moon that night,
though the frost was cruel,
when a poor man came in sight,
gathering winter fuel.

© Copyright 1997 Kevin Mayhew Ltd.
It is illegal to photocopy music.

SLEIGH BELLS

* *The right hand should be played an octave higher than written.*